Curly Crow

Goes to the Balloon Festival
Adventures of a Crow Pilot

Written by
Nicholas Aragon

Illustrated by
Natalia Junqueira

ISBN: 978-1-957701-23-3 (Hardback)
978-1-957701-24-0 (Paperback)
978-1-957701-25-7 (Ebook)

Library of Congress Control Number: 2023930032

Printed by Curly Crow in the United States of America.

first edition 2023.

support@curlycrow.com
Albuquerque, New Mexico

www.CurlyCrow.com

I dedicate this book to the breathtaking skies of New Mexico and the Balloon festival that painted my childhood with wonder, this book is dedicated to the memories that still float in my heart. May its pages carry the spirit of those colorful balloons, inspiring children to reach for their dreams as they soar through life's adventures. With heartfelt appreciation to the enchanting landscapes and cherished moments that shaped my Albuquerque upbringing, this book is a tribute to the magic of hot air balloons and the love they continue to ignite.

Nicholas Aragon

Curly Crow is the happiest—and most curious—little crow ever! She lives with her family in New Mexico, right next to a café. Mmmmm...it smells so good! The Crow family loves having their delicious meals from the café's overflowing dumpster.

"Dad," Curly asks one bright October morning, "can we do something fun this weekend?"

"Yeah, Dad! Can we do something really, really, really fun?" asks little sister, as she lifts her head out of the dumpster with a fish in her beak.

Dad smiles. "How would you like to go to the Balloon festival?" "Yes!" Curly shouts. "I love hot air balloons! I mean I love to look at them. I'm afraid to go up so high, so I'll just enjoy them from the ground."

"I wish I were brave enough to ride in one of those balloons" she says with a sigh.

"Well, guess what!" says Dad. This year, we will be riding in the crow-shaped balloon!" Curly pretends to be excited, but she keeps thinking, They go so, so high!

Over the next few days, Curly's family members from all over the country arrive for the festival. Curly is excited to see her Gramma, her favorite auntie, and her cousins.

With the balloon festival in town all week, the dumpsters are full of delicious food. They are all a bit smelly, but the crows love smelly food!

On the first day of the balloon festival, Curly's dad calls everyone into the kitchen. "I have an announcement," he says. "Curly Crow is invited to be a Crow Pilot this year!"

Curly is excited and afraid at the same time. "I can't believe it!" she says. "I have never been a Crow Pilot before. I have never even been on a balloon ride!" "Wow, Dad," she says. "This will be the adventure of a lifetime!"

On the morning of the festival, the Crow family wakes up early so they can get to the field before the sun comes up. When they arrive, the field is filled with thousands of other birds and hundreds of balloons. They see every color of the rainbow.

Curly is amazed to see the many gift stands, snack bars, and even a coffee and hot cocoa shop set up in the field. But she is most excited to see that there are dumpsters EVERYWHERE!

"I'll stay down here and eat while the rest of you go up high. I'll wave to you," she says.

Dad sees Curly eyeing the dumpsters and says, "Don't worry, Curly. We will feast as soon as the flight is over, I promise."

Dad understands her fear of heights. "You can do this, Curly!" he says. "I know you can!"

Birds of all shapes and sizes begin to fill the balloons with hot air. Soon the balloons begin to rise. The Crow family makes their way across the field to the one balloon that's shaped like a big crow.

"Are you my Crow Pilot?" asks a weathered-looking crow standing in the balloon's basket. Curly looks at Dad's big smile, then bravely replies, "Yes I am, sir!" She jumps into the basket. "I'm ready," she says. "Let's do it!"

The balloon basket is big enough to hold the entire Crow family. As they lift off, the balloon rises higher and higher until it is **3,000 feet high**. Crows can only fly up to **1,000 feet**, so the view is fantastic.

Curly's sister points down and shouts, "Look! That's our house and the café! I can even see our dumpster!" At first, Curly is afraid to look down, but she sees Dad smiling at her, and she bravely looks over the side of the basket. I CAN do this, she says to herself.

When Curly notices that they are floating closer and closer to the Rio Grande River, she lets the pilot know. "Ok, Crow Pilot," he says, "let's see if we can splash and dash." Seconds later, the bottom of their basket skims the top of the river.

The pilot pumps more hot air into the balloon and they rise up, up, up once again. Everyone laughs. The Crow family will remember this day forever.

With Curly's help, the pilot circles back, returns to the field, and lands the balloon perfectly. As they touch down, Curly's stomach rumbles so loudly that everyone hears it!

"Looks like it's time to get to a dumpster," Dad says. When they thank the pilot for the amazing ride, he turns to Curly and says, "You can return any time you wish, Curly Crow. You are the best Crow Pilot I have ever had!"

GRRRr

After a long day of fun, the Crow family finds a dumpster filled with yummy foods like breakfast burritos and donuts. They enjoy their meal and talk about how much fun they had at the Balloon festival. Curly Crow is feeling happy—and brave. The family agrees that they will do this again next year!

About the Author

Nicholas Aragon is an avid hot air balloon enthusiast who has been captivated by these magnificent flying vessels since his childhood. Attending balloon festivals has been an annual tradition for him, as he eagerly embraces the vibrant colors and graceful dance of balloons taking flight. Despite his lifelong passion for hot air balloons, he has never pursued becoming a pilot himself. Nevertheless, his love for these majestic aircraft fuels his unwavering dedication to the world of hot air ballooning.

Albuquerque, New Mexico

Nicholas Aragon has a graduate degree in Higher Education Administration. His vast experience working with children satisfies his deep passion for helping to change lives, one student at a time. In addition to his children's books, he also creates and sells Curly Crow art and apparel. Nicholas resides in New Mexico with his wife and two daughters.

To find out when the next Curly Crow book will be released, please visit our website: https://www.curlycrow.com/book-shop/ and sign up to join our email list. You can also follow Curly Crow on Instagram: https://www.instagram.com/curlycrowbooks/

Printed in the USA
CPSIA information can be obtained
at www.ICGtesting.com
LVHW071526010923
756894LV00002B/2

9 781957 701233